# MALTON, OLD MALTON & NORTON

## THROUGH TIME

John T. Stone

AMBERLEY PUBLISHING

Lower end of Wentworth Street, Malton. This postcard was posted on 27 May 1906.

First published 2009

Amberley Publishing Plc
Cirencester Road, Chalford,
Stroud, Gloucestershire, GL6 8PE

www.amberley-books.com

Copyright © John T. Stone, 2009

The right of John T. Stone to be identified as the
Author of this work has been asserted in accordance
with the Copyrights, Designs and Patents Act 1988.

ISBN 978 1 84868 518 5

British Library Cataloguing in Publication Data.
A catalogue record for this book is available from
the British Library.

Typeset in 9.5pt on 12pt Celeste.
Typesetting by Amberley Publishing.
Printed in the UK.

# Introduction

People are fascinated by change, and intrigued by changes in the local environment. The purpose of this book is to invite the reader to explore what happened to places over the last century. In some cases recent construction of buildings and the growth of trees have altered the old picture considerably. Edwardian streets look different from today's, with the total absence of motor cars.

This book illustrates the changes that have taken place in Malton, Norton and Old Malton over the years. Many changes have occurred due to the demolishing of buildings and total streets. The towns have a chequered history starting many years ago with the Parisi Stone Age settlement. In the year AD 71 Romans invaded and built a fort called Derventio – being the oldest town-fort north of the Humber – and departed in AD 429. The Saxons had a settlement and called it Meldun. In the Domesday Book it is recorded as Maltune which refers to Old Malton Village.

A wooden castle was built near to the Roman fort, and in 1135 Archbishop Thurstan's army besieged and burnt it and the neighbouring houses to the ground. Eustace Fitz-John built a stone castle and also walled the town and it was then called New Malton. He gave his Old Malton Manor to the Canons of the Gilbertine Order. St Mary's parish church is all that remains of the priory. Reigning monarchs visited the castle; Richard I, John and Edward II. In 1322 Robert the Bruce occupied it, and then the castle fell in to ruins.

The estate was then owned by the Eure family and they built a house on the site in 1569. It was replaced in 1604. Later it became the property of two sisters who could not agree on ownership, so in 1674 the High Sheriff of Yorkshire came. He decided the best thing to do was to divide the house, so he had it demolished, but he decided to spare the Lodge Gatehouse. Later in time it was converted into two houses and then to the present Old Lodge Hotel. The site of the castles and houses in the year 2008 was open to the public as a wildlife park called Castle Gardens.

The estate was sold to Sir Thomas Wentworth in 1712. It then passed to Earl Fitzwilliam in 1782 and remains in his family to this day. In 1643 King Charles I and Queen Henrietta stayed here. In the eighteenth and nineteenth century vessels used the Derwent, taking goods to the West Riding. The railway arrived in 1845, bringing the industrial age with it.

Breweries and mills were established; Walker & Dunlop's brewery in 1767, then it was taken over by Chas Rose & Co. Derwent Brewery arrived in 1771, owned by the Russells, and in 1823 they went into partnership with Mr Wilby, owner of the flour mill. In 1897 they also went into partnership with William Wrangham of the Crystal Brewery and became known as Russell & Wrangham. Through time it was taken over by Camerons who later sold the site which then became a supermarket.

The cattle market (fat stock and store) flourished and is still operational to this day. Norton in the 1700s was one of the largest racehorse centres in the north with its own racecourse. The famous trainer John Scott trained at Whitewall Stables in the mid-nineteenth century and his horses won the 2,000 Guineas, the Derby and the St Ledger. Race horse training is still carried out and an important local industry.

You are invited to study the pictures on the following pages which give us an insight in to the times of our ancestors.

John T. Stone

# Old Malton

**Old Malton**
Town Street, the thatched cottages on the right-hand side have all been demolished and modern half-timbered houses built in their place. On the old picture, below the telegraph pole was the post office.

### St Mary's Church
St Mary the Virgin was part of the Priory founded between 1147 and 1153, and it was given to the Canons of the Gilbertine Order, by Eustace Fitz-John. This was the original village of Malton or in the Doomsday Book 'MALTUNE' (1086).

**Town Street**

The Royal Oak was a beer house in 1840 and was licensed in 1896. Looking right we see the chapel, now converted in to St Mary's Priory Church Community Centre, next to the War Memorial Hall and then another chapel, with the school behind now turned into dwellings.

## Westgate

The Wentworth Arms was named after the Wentworth Family, who were Lords of the Manor until 1782. The village pump stood near the gas light, both have now been removed. The thatched cottage and one other are all that survive today.

## Old Malton Mill

This was the site of Mr Hurtley's water mill in 1846, as a result of the Rye and Derwent Drainage Act, the course of the river was changed so the mill lost its water power. They relocated to Railway Street, Malton, until 1885, when they moved to Hull, except one of the brothers who remained in the house.

The Abbey House, Old Malton
The rest home was the family home of the Walker family. In earlier years this was the home of Mr Smithson who moved from Easthorpe Hall. He was a great friend of Charles Dickens who visited him here. Charles Dickens modelled Scrooge's office in his story *A Christmas Carol* on Mr Smithson's office in Chancery Lane, Malton.

# Malton

### Orchard Fields
This is the site of the Roman fort; the plinth stands where the corner of the fort was. The Romans came to Malton in the year AD 71 and stayed until AD 429.

## Orchard Fields

During the excavations, this Roman villa was discovered in 1949. The west end of the floor is in fair condition and shows a hunting dog in the centre with panels on either side. The four panels are thought to represent the four seasons. Winter shows a man dressed for the cold weather holding a leafless branch, and is the only remaining panel at the corner of the room.

## The Estate Office
This is the headquarters of the Earl Fitzwilliam Estate. Here you would have paid your tolls when bringing livestock to market. Lower down are the outer walls of the Lodge.

## Lodge Gateways
The outer wall of the entrance to the gatehouse and mansion. The three gateways and the Lodge survive.

## The Lodge

The Old Lodge gardens were owned by two houses, later made in the Lodge Hotel. The pathway leads down to the new Castle Garden Park, which was opened to the public in 2008.

The Lodge Malton (South)

### The Lodge Hotel

Behind the Lodge is the site of the castle and two houses, and now the site has been converted into Castle Gardens for the use of the people of Malton. Lord Eure built houses on the site. The last one was built in 1604 which was later inherited in 1674 by two sisters. They could not agree ownership so, after a court case, the High Sheriff of Yorkshire reduced the house into two piles of stones.

St. Leonards Church, Malton.

### St Leonard's Church

This twelfth century chapel of ease called St Leonard's was connected to the Old Malton Priory of St Mary's. On 5 December 1768 eight bells were hung. The present tower was erected in 1860. The clock marks Queen Victoria's Jubilee in 1897, and was a gift from Earl Fitzwilliam. Church services are still being held by the Roman Catholic community.

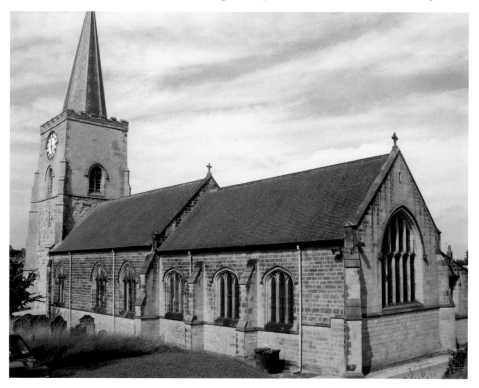

## Greengate

All the houses have been demolished and St Leonard's Close stands on the site. In the centre of the picture the Elephant and Castle public house can be seen.

## Greengate School

This Wesleyan School was built in 1837. Pupils from the age of seven to eleven were taught here in Greengate. The oldest part of the school has been demolished.

## Greengate

Looking up Greengate to the Wesleyan School. It was built in 1837 and has been partly demolished. On the left-hand side stood the Elephant and Castle public house, which in 1840 was a beer house. It closed in 1951, and Greengate flats were erected on the site. On the right-hand side was Victoria Square.

## Greengate

Looking down Greengate; in the centre of the picture stands the Elephant and Castle public house, which closed in 1951. The first house on the right-hand side was the home of Charles Dickens' brother, Alfred Lambert Dickens, who was an engineer for the Malton and Scarborough line, and who Charles often visited.

## Old Maltongate

All the houses on the right-hand side have been demolished to widen the road at Post Office Corner, now known as Butcher Corner. St Leonard's flats are built on part of the site. On the left-hand side the inn sign of the eighteenth-century White Swan public house can be seen.

## Post Office Corner or Butcher Corner

In 1967, better access was required for motor cars turning in to Castlegate so Snow's shop and the Castlegate Vaults public house, which got its licence in 1890 and closed in 1965, were demolished for the road widening. The road down Yorkersgate turning into Castlegate was part of the A64 from York to Scarborough. The shop was owned by the Snow family from 1826.

## Yorkersgate

Looking down Yorkersgate to Post Office Corner. On the right-hand side is a coaching inn. Originally called the Black Horse and built in 1720 the name was changed to the George in about 1845. It was both a coaching and a carriers' inn. The archway leads to Water Lane, now Railway Street car park, and the lane goes down to the river. More rooms were required by the George in the 1880s, and an archway was thrown over to add these rooms. Horses were taken down to the river for water and to wash their legs. Opposite was Dodsworth's shop, timber was brought by boat and was delivered up Water Lane direct into their workshops.

### Saville Street

Anderson's sport shop stands on the site of the Temperance Hotel; Mr William Small was a tenant in 1893. Beyond the shops is the Wesleyan Methodist Chapel, built in 1811 with 700 seats. Further on, the Congregation Chapel was built in 1815 with 450 seats. It is now up for commercial rent.

### Looking Up Yorkersgate

On the left-hand side you can see the *Malton Gazette* office. Further up was Longster's seed merchants.

## Yorkersgate

This was part of the A64 road from York to Scarborough. On the left-hand side are Pearsons & Ward solicitors' offices, below was the White Horse Inn, founded in the seventeenth century and closed in 1859. It became a boys' school and later the doctors' surgery. On the right-hand side we have York House and behind the tree you can see a house which is now demolished.

## Market Street

Looking down Market Street we have, on the right-hand side, the Green Man Hotel, and also the Fleece public house which is now part of the Green Man. Below was the Old Talbot Hotel. At the bottom of the street York House can be seen.

## York House

York House has occupied its H-plan footprint since at least the fifteenth century, and is a stone house that incorporates elements of an earlier timber-frame house on the site. It was raised up in the late sixteenth century and substantially altered and improved in the late seventeenth century by Sir William Strickland and Eure family heiress, Elizabeth Palmes who married in 1684. Most of what is seen today is as they left it. The house was sold to the Wentworth-Watsons in 1739. The orange, copperas pigmented limewash is as used on the house in the eighteenth century. Much of the town was limewashed this colour, which was, in effect, the 'Estate colour' of the time. Limewash protects against decay.

### Talbot Hotel

It was built in 1684 by Sir William Strickland as a Hunting Lodge, and was bought by the Hon. Thomas Watson-Wentworth, Earl of Malton, in 1739, and opened as an inn during 1742. The Talbot had a horse-drawn bus between the hotel and the railway station. If the bus was at the railway station and was needed, a horn was blown from the terrace, which overlooked the railway station and the River Derwent, telling the driver he and the bus were needed for the next customer. Some of the medieval town wall survives in the basement levels.

## St Michael's School

Built in 1865/6, Misses Spence and Misses Halls moved their young ladies' school from The Cloisters. It was originally called Prospect House, and later became St Michael's School. It closed at the beginning of the Second World War and was then turned into an hotel. Sadly it is now closed.

**The Mount**
This was a private road, and the gates had to be locked for one day each year.

The War Memorial, Malton.

## Top of Yorkersgate

On the site behind the war memorial stood the Russian Cannon, which originally stood in the Market Place and was moved here in 1883. It was captured at the battle of Sebastopol in 1855 during the Crimean War and was gifted to the town. Later a German gun was added. The guns and iron railings were removed for scrap during the Second World War.

## Castle Howard Road

This road leads to the stately home Castle Howard. The housing estate on the right-hand side occupies the site of Longster's gardens and orchards, and it was also the playing field of St Michael's Girls' School. The only remaining relic of the orchard is a holm oak tree which was planted at the entrance gate.

## York Road

Part of the turnpike road which ran from York to Scarborough. A new housing estate called Rockingham Close is on the right-hand side, just after the older larger houses.

## Lower Wheelgate

Humphreys & Son, grocers, are next door to the Yorkshire Penny Bank. Later, Iles Dress Shop was incorporated in the bank, and Humphreys was taken over by Currys, which has now closed.

## Wheelgate

In the 1930s, the Sun Inn of eighteenth-century origin run by Mr Spanton was demolished and a Woolworth's and an outfitters were built on the site. Galtry's Outfitters is now the Halifax Building Society.

WHEELGATE, MALTON.

Nº 1010.

### Wheelgate

Fentress supply store and the Yorkshire Penny Bank on the left became the C.W.S. Later the building was converted into a drug store and then the Yorkshire Trading Company. In the centre of the picture you can see Russell's Chimney and also Snow's shop which was demolished for road widening in 1967.

## Wheelgate

Here we have Mr Horsley's cycle depot, next door is Mr Heyne's butcher's shop, lower down are some small shops which were later demolished and the post office was built on the site. A traveller's cart stands outside of the Leeds Clothing Co. On the right-hand side the pillars and stairs to the Primitive Methodist Chapel can be seen, which was demolished in 1951. Today, cars are parked where carts once stood.

## St Michael's Street

Leatham's Boot Mart is still a shoe shop today. The building on the left-hand side was modernised and became a gents' outfitters but changed hands many times and is now a butcher's shop. The houses halfway up the street and the National School, built in 1857, were demolished to make way for Malton Library.

## Primitive Chapel

The chapel was built in 1866 with seats to hold 650 people. In the basement they ran a youth club, but sadly it was demolished in 1951 to make way for shops. The shops now occupying the site are Stead & Simpson, a travel agents and St Catherine's charity shop.

WHEELGATE MALTON 1

## Wheelgate

A saddler's shop is still on the site of Mr Wardill's shop. The Clarence public house, now closed, was a dram shop in 1860 and got its name in 1892. Now, in 2009 it is has reopened with its name changed to the Jockey.

### Finkle Street

The Prince of Wales Hotel was a beer house in the 1850s. It became a hotel in 1870 and was closed in the 1920s. In 1935 it was demolished along with the Elizabethan Sessions house. Bowers café was built on the corner, which catered for weddings and dances and is now Boyes Store. On the left-hand side stood the town lock up, which is now an opening to the shops' car park.

## Newbiggin

We are looking up Newbiggin, and this road goes to Helmsley. Houses were built outside the town wall; as it was a new beginning this is how it got its name. The road on the right-hand side leads to Princess Road. The white building just above is the Blue Ball public house, which was Harrison's Folly in 1705 and became the Blue Ball in 1823.

## Newbiggin

This view looking down Newbiggin has not altered; only the cars are more modern.

### Broughton Rise

Looking down Newbiggin to St Leonard's Church, on the left-hand side is Sparrow Park, most of the trees have been removed for road widening and traffic lights have been installed. The toll gate stood here, and an official collected the tolls for animals coming into the market.

## Middlecave Road

Up this road you will find Malton Hospital and the Old Grammar School, which is now called Malton School.

**Lower Middlecave**

The houses and shops were removed, Spitalfield Court was built and the road widened. The Adult School and Pioneer Club can be seen on the right-hand side, which is now the site of Sainsbury's supermarket.

## Cemetery Road

Later called Princess Road. The trees form the avenue down to the cemetery and behind them was Woodall's Roper Walk, which was used in making ropes. After the row of terrace houses was a building, which was originally the Cottage Hospital (1905).

## Princess Road

Malton Cottage Hospital was built (1905) with ten beds and two cots and just one matron and two nurses. Later, it became the British Legion Club. In 1925, the Princess Royal came and opened it and they changed the name of the road to Princess Mary's Road, and eventually Princess Road. The building was demolished and flats (Princess Court) were built on the site.

## Cattle Market

In the year 1826 the cattle market was moved to this site by Earl Fitzwilliam, who also built a slaughter house. The houses were removed and it became the site for sheep pens.

## Cattle Market

The Spotted Cow was a beer house in 1807 and later got its licence in 1869. Next door was the police station, built in 1893. The rest of the premises have been made into the sheep market. The cattle pens and offices still remain.

## Victoria Road

Malton Police Station and Court House, built in 1900 for the cost of £1,200, were situated on this road, in the red brick building on the left-hand side. The building in the centre of the picture was originally a clay pipe factory.

**Market Square**
Looking up to the town hall, built in the sixteenth century, this covered market had a Justices' Room above. This was the site of the cattle market until 1826 when Earl Fitzwilliam moved it to its present site. A Saturday market is held here every week.

## Town Hall

The town hall was a covered market with the Justices' Room above. It was remodelled in 1856, but in 1877 partly destroyed by fire. Now is used by Malton Roman Museum and the Tourist Board.

### St Michael's Church

A twelfth-century chapel of ease, belonging to the Old Malton Priory. Here you can see the Butter Market with stalls and carriers' carts. Also can be seen the first gas light to be lit in 1836.

## Fitch's Shop

At the bottom side of the Market Place was Fitch's & Co. It was a milliner's shop and employed a good many Malton people. The building on the left-hand side is the Balloon Yeast Stores – now an estate agents – and the Royal Oak public house can also be seen.

## Castlegate

Looking up the street, on the right-hand side the road called Church Hill enters Castlegate. The houses on both side of the road are now demolished.

## Castlegate

Hodgson & Broadbent's shop and Pickering's cake shop next door were at the top of Russell's Yard. The smaller building next door is now a ladies' hairdressers. All the shops and Russell & Wrangham's Brewery and Flour Mills have gone now to make way for a Morrison's supermarket.

## Mill Cottages, Sheep's Foot Hill

The workers of the Malton Estate Co. lived in this row of cottages. At the end of the row was King's Mill, which has been converted into flats. On the left-hand side was the workhouse. Now the fire station and a playgroup occupy the site.

## Riverside

This view shows Owston Warehouse in Navigation Wharf. This building is now being restored to bring it back to its original state. Behind the wall and trees was Water Lane and the rifle range, which have now been converted into Railway Street car park.

## Russell's From The River

Derwent Brewery arrived in 1771, which was owned by the Russell family. In 1823 they took over the Flour Mill, and in 1897 went into partnership with William Wrangham and became Russell and Wrangham. It was sold in 1958 to Melbourne Breweries of Leeds, later Camerons owned it and sold the site for a supermarket. The Russell and Wrangham buildings and shops in Castlegate were demolished in 1984 and the supermarket was built.

Railway Bridge, Malton

## Railway Bridge

When the railway arrived, a wooden bridge was built for Malton people to reach the station in 1845. Later, it was replaced by an iron bridge in 1870, for a branch line to cross over with goods to the Malton Biscuit Co. Mill.

**Malton Railway Station**

The railway arrived in 1845. Malton station had a central platform for trains going to York. A bogie was pulled out from under the platform so passengers could cross over for the York train, but sadly this has been removed. Lines also went to Whitby, Driffield and Thirsk from here.

# Norton-on-Derwent

### County Bridge
The River Derwent was the dividing line between the North & East Ridings of Yorkshire. This view is of the East Riding side.

## Footbridge over the Railway
The railway footbridge was taken down in the 1980s. The gasometer has also been removed.

## Railway Crossings

There were four large gates, and two small ones through which you could pass after the larger ones had been closed. This view shows the old wooden gates and the footbridge which was removed in the late 1980s. The man on the left-hand side has got a stalk table on a hand cart. In the centre of the picture are the mills in Castlegate and the church clock. All that remains in the modern picture is St Leonard's church clock.

Church St, Norton, Malton.

### Lower Church Street

The Majestic cinema was demolished and later the site became a petrol filling station. On the left-hand side was Mr Bower's garage, but before that it was the Norton Court House and police station. Built by the Magistrates of East Yorkshire in 1858, they moved out in the early 1900s. Now the building has been demolished.

## Church Street

The house and forge on the right-hand side belonged to Mr Boyce, blacksmith, and later Mr Nesfield took over. This building and two other shops were demolished to widen the road and to make a road to the car park.

## Church Street

Behind the trees stands the swimming baths. They are on the site of St Nicholas's Church. The medieval church was on this site until 1814, when it was demolished and a new church was built. This survived until 1900. Later, the swimming baths were built, which were originally open air and opened to the public on 26 September 1902.

## St Nicholas's Church

This medieval church was on the site on which the swimming baths were built. St Nicholas was the patron saint of wayfarers. It was demolished in 1814. A Grecian-style church was built and, in 1891, the final services were held, then it was demolished in 1901. The services were moved to the new church of St Peter.

## Railway Hotel

In 1850 it changed its name from the Bay Horse to the Railway Hotel. This view has not altered very much.

## The Buckrose Hotel

This was originally a row of shops including Mr Spanton's chemist shop and, in 1899, a Mr Searle had them demolished and built new shops and the Buckrose Hotel on the site.

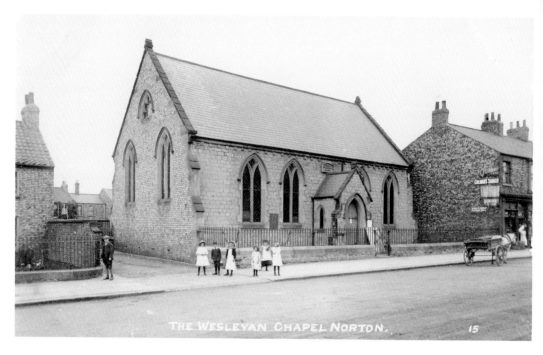

THE WESLEYAN CHAPEL NORTON. 15

## Trinity Chapel

In 2002, a fire which was started by an electrical fault in the organ damaged the inside of the chapel. With the help of many dedicated people it is now a beautiful place to worship. The original chapel was opened on Tuesday 16 February 1858 and the Rev Richard Roberts from Leeds was invited to preach the opening sermon. Trinity has now celebrated 150 years.

## Bethal Chapel

Piccadilly was the name of the area of land and was sold for £140 12s 6d, Bethel Chapel was built on the site and the stone-laying took place on Thursday 31 March 1864.

Commercial Street, Norton

MALTON

### Norton Court House

The court house and police station were built in the late 1890s. Norton Boys' School stood next door. It was later demolished and the library built on the site. The court house is now the home of Norton-on-Derwent Town Council and the police station has been converted into flats.

## Scarborough Road

This road was once part of the old A64. The inn on the left-hand side was called the Blue Bell. After 1857 it was renamed Balaclava after the Battle of Balaclava and was closed in 1972. It later became Priorpot House.

## Scarborough Road

This picture shows Priorpot Bridge and the road on the left to the Mill Hill laundry. On its site stands Rivermead nursing home. This bridge has now been widened and on the right a new housing estate now exists.

## Mill Street

Originally called Green Lane, this was the site of Victoria Windmill which was owned by Mr Lovall. The name was later changed to Mill Street in 1857.

## Little Wood Street

At the end of Little Wood Street, the original Hyde Park public house can be seen. On the left-hand side stands Wellington House which was used by the doctors for their surgery.

## Wood Street

This street is about the same except for the removal of some houses. The Salvation Army Citadel is on the site of the liberal club. Off Wood Street is Grove Street, at the end of which Norton Girls' School was built and is now the primary school.

**Beverley Road**

Wood Street and Mill Street converge to form Beverley Road. This road leads to Driffield, Beverley and Hull.

## Housing Estate

This view of the new housing estate is taken looking to Howe Road and The Grove. The shop is still a newsagents, next to Norton cleaners and Hanley's greengrocers.

### Eastfield

Eastfield Model Farm council estate was built in the 1940s. The view is looking up Dean Road, and St Peter's church tower can be seen in the centre of the picture.

## Jubilee Road

Jubilee Road is one of many council estates in Norton-on-Derwent.

**Wold Road**
Wold Road now named Langton Road. This row of cottages stands at the top of St Nicholas Street.

## Langton Road

Originally this was called Wold Road, leading to the village of Langton. On the left-hand side, behind the tree, was the football field, now the site of a housing estate called St Peter's Crescent. The fencing on the right-hand side was later replaced with wrought iron railings. The far end house of the terrace on the right was a public house called the Rifleman's Arms, which closed in 1900.

**St Peter Street**
Looking up to Langton Road, these rows of Victorian houses all had wrought iron railings that were removed in the Second World War for the war effort.

## Sutton Street

On the centre of the land in Sutton Street stood a racing stable, which was demolished and new houses added to the other houses. The old postcard was sent from No. 37, which is the house marked with an X.

### St Peter's Church

The old church of St Nicholas in Church Street became too small for the community so a new church had to be built. Mr Wyse gave the site in 1889, and the foundation stone was laid in 1894. It was enlarged and the tower was added later, in stages. It was completed in 1909 in memory of King Edward Vll.

## Welham Road

The road way was about half the width, and the other half being a ford through which you could take a horse and cart. Bark Knots came from Rustons & Priestmans' tan yard in Castlegate. In front of this mound ran the open stream from Beck Mills and it entered a tunnel under the railway into the River Derwent. On the left-hand side was C. E. Mennell & Son's sawmills later it became Taylor Bros. After that it became a clothing factory and a housing estate called Springfield Garth. Now, it could soon be the site of a supermarket.

## Beck Mills

This water mill was listed in the Domesday Book. The pond was later used as a trout hatchery. Sadly, the mill was demolished, the pond landscaped, and a bungalow built in the same style as the water mill. The site is now part of a new housing estate.

## Welham Road

This view looking down Welham Road shows green fields on either side and a view of St Leonard's church clock from Whitewall. Now, all that can be seen are rows of houses.

WELHAM R^D NORTON                                    49

## Welham Road

This view is taken from the bottom of Whitewall looking towards St Peter's Church. After the extensive development of houses, this view is lost for ever.

## Whitewall

The famous racehorse trainer, Mr John Scott, trained here at Whitewall Stables. He died on 4 October 1871 aged seventy-six. His horses won sixteen St Ledgers, six Derbys, eight Oaks, eight Two Thousand and four One Thousand Guineas – an amazing record never since equalled. He trained, at times, eighty to one hundred horses, including the celebrated racehorse, Blink Bonny. This racehorse won the Derby and Oaks Stakes at Epsom in 1857, was owned and bred by William I'Anson and ridden by J. Charlton.

Malton from the River Derwent showing the biscuit factory and riverside warehouses.

# Acknowledgements

I would like to thank my family for their help and patience, especially my son Christopher and my daughter Catherine and her husband David Hyder, without whose help this book might not have been published. I would also like to thank Mrs Rosemary Netzel and Mr Nigel Copley.